How to Be a Friend

Fabiola Sepulveda

Notes for the Grown-ups

This wordless book allows for a rich shared reading experience for children who do not yet know how to read words or who are beginning to learn. Children can look at the pages to gather information from what they see, and they can suggest text to tell the story.

To extend this reading experience, do one or more of the following:

Discuss what makes a good friend.

Introduce vocabulary such as these words when looking at the pictures and telling the story you see:

- bring
- choose
- comfort
- friend
- fun

- help
- introduce
- kind
- meet
- play

- share
- talk
- together
- turns
- us

Tell the child about your best friend and what makes them so special to you. Ask the child to tell you the same.

After reading the pictures, come back to the book again and again. Rereading is an excellent tool for building literacy skills.

Encourage the child to draw a picture of themselves and a friend doing something they love to do.

Consultant

Cynthia Malo, M.A.Ed.

Publishing Credits

Rachelle Cracchiolo, M.S.Ed., *Publisher*
Emily R. Smith, M.A.Ed., *SVP of Content Development*
Véronique Bos, *VP of Creative*
Dona Herweck Rice, *Senior Content Manager*

Image Credits: all images from iStock and/or Shutterstock

Library of Congress Cataloging-in-Publication Data

Names: Sepulveda, Fabiola, author.
Title: How to be a friend / Fabiola Sepulveda.
Description: Huntington Beach, CA : Teacher Created Materials, Inc, 2024. |
  Audience: Ages 3-9. | Summary: In a book without words, it is clear that
  the best way to get a friend is simply to be a friend.
Identifiers: LCCN 2024007609 (print) | LCCN 2024007610 (ebook) | ISBN
  9798765961247 (paperback) | ISBN 9798765967461 (ebook)
Subjects: LCSH: Friendship--Juvenile fiction. | Friendship--Pictorial
  works. | Stories without words. | CYAC: Friendship--Fiction. | Stories
  without words. | LCGFT: Picture books.
Classification: LCC PZ7.1.S4625 Ho 2024 (print) | LCC PZ7.1.S4625 (ebook)
  | DDC [E]--dc23/eng/20240314
LC record available at https://lccn.loc.gov/2024007609
LC ebook record available at https://lccn.loc.gov/2024007610

TCM Teacher Created Materials

5482 Argosy Avenue
Huntington Beach, CA 92649
www.tcmpub.com
ISBN 979-8-7659-6124-7
© 2025 Teacher Created Materials, Inc.
Printed by: 926. Printed in: Malaysia. PO#: PO11723